All About
ACADEMY MEMBERSHIP

All About
ACADEMY MEMBERSHIP

Your Guide to the BEST KEPT SECRETS for
Building an Estate Planning Law Firm

As of January 2016

> The American Academy of Estate
> Planning Attorneys presents a complete
> explanation of Member benefits, services,
> and tools in this comprehensive book
> about Academy Membership.

Written by the founders of The American Academy of Estate
Planning Attorneys and co-authors of *The E-Myth Attorney*

ROBERT ARMSTRONG and SANFORD M. FISCH

Acknowledgements

We'd like to acknowledge *you*.

It's refreshing to discover attorneys who are interested in thriving, not just surviving. We find that attorneys who request these materials are entrepreneurial by nature and always looking for new ideas, new tools, and new ways to take their practice to the next level.

Nothing pleases us more than being able to contribute to the success of the owners of estate planning and elder law firms.

If you would like a free copy of our eBook, *"11 Essential Systems: A Guide to Creating a Thriving Law Firm and a Satisfying Life,"* simply email **info@aaepa.com** and request that the download be sent to you.

Table of Contents

ROBERT ARMSTRONG and SANFORD M. FISCH,
Founders of the American Academy of Estate Planning
Attorneys and co-authors of *The E-Myth Attorney*

FROM THE BEGINNING, WE'VE BEEN CLEAR IN OUR MISSION

In the early years of running our own law practices, we experienced what it was like to cobble together the systems and tools we needed to reach the success we ultimately achieved. We had to learn the hard way when it came to running a practice and becoming the expert estate planning attorneys in our community. We realized how little preparation law school offers for the real world challenges of running a business. Law school taught us how to do the legal work, but there were no classes on how to hire and train employees, how to market our services, or how to create memorable experiences for our clients. Our desire to master these business skills and help other attorneys do the same made our vision crystal clear.

Since 1993, our driving mission has been to inspire attorneys to look at their law practices differently. As our Members began to see that a law firm could be both a professional practice and a thriving business, they saw their income increase, their work / life balance improve and a new awareness arose that practicing law could be fun again.

WE WANTED A BETTER WAY TO PRACTICE LAW, SO WE CREATED IT

Our dream was, and still is, centered around creating and delivering tools, systems, education, and coaching to attorneys who shouldn't have to reinvent that wheel.

In the pages that follow, we will highlight some of the tools and services that make Academy Members the premier estate planning and elder law attorneys in their communities. Please take your time in perusing the information in this book. Review it during a quiet time where you can envision your future and try on a few of the ideas. Oftentimes, as we've discussed thoroughly in the book we co-authored with Michael E. Gerber, *The E-Myth Attorney*, practice owners get so immersed in the daily needs of the practice, the team members, or the clients, that they rarely set aside time to work "on" the business.

WE CHALLENGE YOU TO DREAM OF AN EASIER WAY TO ACHIEVE YOUR GOALS

If your practice isn't quite where you envisioned it would be by now or if you're changing gears in some way, take the time to specifically and strategically visualize exactly the practice you want in your future. Getting from here to there will always require something you haven't had access to before. We hope you'll call and visit with various Academy Members and ask them about the practice and the life they dreamed of and what it took to attain that level of fulfillment.

KNOW WHY YOU DO WHAT YOU DO

We help our Members rediscover the "why" of their practice and seize the opportunity to be a contribution not only to clients and team members, but to their community. All of this adds up to a new sense of purpose of what it means to practice law.

You don't have to be an Academy Member to get in touch with "why" you're an attorney, or "why" you have a law practice. Once you're clear, your path becomes easier. It can guide every part of your life, from the choices you make on how you conduct business, which clients you decide to work with, and what meaningful impact you and your firm have on others.

BE SELECTIVE IN THE COMPANY YOU KEEP

Keep in mind, there is another choice you make each day that impacts your success. That is the choice of "who." It is the conduit of who you want to become, who you want to impact, and who has an impact on you. Stop and ask yourself, "Who do I need to be to perform at my best and who should I associate with and be influenced by to reach my goals?" Harvard professor, David McClelland asserts, "Your choice of a reference group will, more than any other factor, determine what happens to you in life."

Simply put, your participation in the Academy puts you in a rare and privileged group by surrounding yourself with like-minded leaders, entrepreneurs, and serious students of success and happiness.

We take great pride in developing a community of attorneys from around the country who inspire and motivate each other to pursue their dreams.

Thank you for the opportunity and privilege to be part of your "who."

To your success,
Robert Armstrong and Sanford M. Fisch

**JENNIFER PRICE, Chief Operating Officer,
American Academy of Estate Planning Attorneys.
Thank you for requesting more information about
Membership in our organization.**

As you may know, "the American Academy" is the most exclusive organization of its kind. Membership can equip you with efficient management systems, cutting-edge software, proven marketing and public relations materials and unparalleled continuing legal education support. Everything an attorney needs to transform all or part of their firm.

Since Membership is limited by geographic area, currently less than 40% of the territories are still available. Only those attorneys who qualify for Membership can be considered as potential Members.

If your territory is still available, you may request a temporary password to visit our private, Members-Only Website. We also urge you to speak directly with several of our Members to hear how Membership has helped change their practices, as well as their lives.

After reviewing everything we've included in this book, most attorneys in your position have a few questions about Membership availability in their area and specifics on how the tools and services actually work to create more time and more revenue for Members.

We try to make it as comfortable as possible for you to email us and set a time aside to talk in more detail about where you are in your practice, what you love about your work, your schedule, your lifestyle, and what you don't.

At the very least, you'll come away from the call with a clearer vision of where you want to take your practice in the coming few years.

I hope that you will get a true picture of how intense the training, tools and support we offer are. Throughout the book, if we have reports or replays of webinars that expand on a given topic, we have included invitations for you to request those additional items.

This book was not designed to be read from cover to cover. You can browse through the table of contents and decide which areas of your practice could use the most support and start your reading wherever you like. Feel free to mark up the book with questions that you can raise when you have a conversation with us or our Members.

I look forward to hearing stories about how some of these ideas or perhaps the invitation to take your investigation of Membership has impacted you.

Looking forward to hearing about your success,

Jennifer Price
Chief Operating Officer
American Academy of Estate Planning Attorneys
(800) 846-1555

OUR HISTORY

The Academy's success started with a book called, *"The E-Myth,"* written by Michael E. Gerber. After building a thriving practice in southern California, we were being approached by attorneys around the country asking about our marketing strategies, about how a law firm could be set up to handle a large volume of estate plans per month and produce that with a high level of quality while developing life-long relationships with clients and their families.

In 1990, we decided to document what we had been creating for years in our own firm. By documenting these time-tested systems, we had the foundation of what would become The American Academy of Estate Planning Attorneys.

Since 1993, when the Academy first made these efficient and quality oriented systems available, attorneys from around the country have been able to deliver unparalleled service to their clients. The Academy serves law firms in over 130 geographic areas in 45 states, and its Members include some of the most widely recognized experts in the estate planning field.

The Academy is still owned by the original founders. Helping us keep the Academy growing and on the cutting edge is a talented, committed collection of professionals experienced in this industry. Most employees and the majority of the Membership have been with the Academy for over 10 years. We have a few staff and Members as well who have been with us over 20 years!

OUR "WHY"

Articulating the Academy's "Why" is always very easy. We do what we do so we can play a role in the transformation of attorneys and law firms around the country.

Because we are so clear about WHY we do what we do, it shapes who we hire. It causes us to be selective with the attorneys we choose to work with. If an attorney simply wants to make more money—that attorney is likely not the best fit for Academy Membership. If the attorney wants something he or she never dreamed was possible in their practice and their life—we stop in our tracks. That's who we are looking for. Those attorneys are why we do what we do.

Transformation impacts all areas of life. You can't transform just your marketing, or just your consultations, or just your relationship with your family. If only one area is impacted, it should be classified as a "change" not a "transformation."

We feel successful when we work with an attorney who worked too many hours, made too little income, had no vacations, or possibly felt guilty about the lack of time available for family... and within a short period of time the same attorney doubles revenue, works a 4-day work week and takes multiple vacations per year.

We've seen it happen. Over and over.

 Go to training.aaepa.com/academyintro for a quick overview of who we are and why we do what we do!

You didn't train for the job of office manager, public relations expert, or computer technician. But in today's world, all those peripheral jobs come with owning your law practice. And it's those constant, time-consuming distractions that keep you from focusing on your clients and your future.

With all these distractions, many of our Members spent years missing out on soccer games and ballet recitals. They didn't have time to play golf or tennis until they learned the skills they needed to have a well-rounded life as well as a thriving practice.

So how do you stay on top of all the demands of a thriving law firm and still have time for a life outside the office? The key is having effective systems in place—and knowing how to use them.

The Academy has structured the systems that must be in place in your firm to achieve true success. Academy support, coaching and tools are centered around these systems.

If you would like more detailed explanation of these 11 Essential Systems, email us and request that we send you our eBook entitled, *"11 Essential Systems: A Guide to Creating a Thriving Law Firm and a Satisfying Life."*

IT'S ABOUT EMPOWERMENT

Our support starts with personalized coaching to help teach you the best practices for law firm success. We walk you through what's worked in the past, and what hasn't. We strive to show you how you can envision your ideal firm, and then make that vision a reality.

With all this in place, you'll be looking at your practice in inspiring new ways. The success of your practice and the achievement of your goals revolves around these **11 ESSENTIAL SYSTEMS:**

SYSTEM 1—STRATEGIC PLANNING SYSTEM
Aligning Your Business with Your Personal Values

Most attorneys operate their law firms with a general direction in mind, but they don't have a written and rewritten plan to achieve specific goals.

Your vision for your firm and for the life you want to lead will determine your personal goals.

Picturing a practice when *"it's done"* with the set-up, when it's working like a charm, and knowing what the details of that image are before beginning is imperative.

The work accomplished at the Academy's Boot Camp leaves every attorney with a solid beginning for a Strategic Plan.

Knowing how many people will be on the team and how many locations a firm will have in three years as well as how much revenue and what services will specifically be offered (or not offered) sets the stage for success.

The process of developing this plan is at the heart of our Member's success stories.

 Be sure to check the Free Stuff section of this book. There are a couple of very good Strategic Planning tools offered on that page.

SYSTEM 2—FINANCE AND OPERATIONS MANAGEMENT SYSTEM
Managing by the Numbers and Seamlessly Making It All Work

The rule of thumb is that you want systems in place that will allow you to review last month's numbers by the 10th of this month... every month. Many Members use QuickBooks, although other software will work fine as well. The Academy established a recommended Chart of Accounts years ago and it continues to come in handy year after year.

Members submit their financials for the prior year during the month of February. All participating Members' financials are entered into a database anonymously and a report is prepared for a private meeting at each Spring Summit.

Can you imagine sitting down with 60-80 actual estate planning law firm financials from the prior year and being able to compare your firm numbers with any other firm from across the country?

Owner's compensation, staff salaries, what you or another Member spent on marketing... all creates the environment for an incredibly open dialogue among Members.

 Once again, check the Free Stuff section of this book. There is a webinar and a handout that goes into detail on some of the financial benchmarks you can use in your firm.

SYSTEM 3—A SYSTEMS APPROACH TO LEADERSHIP
Creating a Firm Culture Focusing on Unique Abilities and the Road to Mastery

A law firm is only as successful as its leadership. The programs, sessions, training and coaching that revolve around taking your leadership to a new level are impossible to list.

Basically every program includes a leadership emphasis. The coaching available on how and when to hire, who you hire, and how you inspire and lead shows up on every coaching call.

For leaders in the Academy who want an even more intense focus on growth in this area, The Peak Performers group may be an option. The Academy co-founders, Robert Armstrong and Sanford Fisch have a quarterly coaching mastermind group of attorneys from within the Membership who gather to explore and expand their limits as leaders.

Knowing your metrics, delegating effectively, and being clear about your own unique abilities as well as those of your team has a dramatic impact on what your firm is capable of achieving.

Those who excel in this area are curious about handling situations in a new way, are coachable and capable of swift execution on a plan.

SYSTEM 4—STAFF ACCOUNTABILITY AND TEAM BUILDING SYSTEM
Putting the Right People with the Right Skills in the Right Positions

The intense number of systems it takes to interview, hire, train, evaluate and occasionally terminate a member of your team is mind boggling.

Unless you're a former employment lawyer, you can get yourself into trouble from time to time without these important systems.

Relying on a Practice Building Coach for advice on the timing of adding a team member as well as the job description and advertising is a great start.

Next, the *"group interviewing"* system alone saves Academy Members hours on the front end. With this system, Member attorneys get the opportunity to evaluate a wide pool of job candidates, while only spending valuable one-on-one time with the most qualified finalists.

The law firm personnel system extends beyond the hiring process and provides support throughout an attorney's relationship with employees. For example, setting up a solid Employee Handbook requires a lot of time that tends to pull attorneys away from client meetings. To save Members time and stress, the Academy provides an easily customizable template. From ads to exit interview forms, training schedules for various positions, and employee handbooks, staffing systems are a key ingredient to your success.

WHAT MEMBERS HAVE TO SAY

"I have always felt that Academy Membership is my secret weapon for success in estate planning! I would not want to attempt to practice in this field without being a Member."

—Iowa Member

SYSTEM 5—COMPREHENSIVE TECHNOLOGY SYSTEM
Leveraging Tools to Draft Documents and Manage Your Firm

Whether you are an Academy Member or not, there are no short cuts to take with technology. When you are looking for tools to handle your firm, make sure you consider how you will:

1. Automate your marketing and client contact
2. Be seen online. What are the initial impressions you'll be giving prospective clients when they search to verify your credibility or to approach you for services

3. Design law firm management reports that reflect the status of each case, show the effectiveness of your marketing efforts, and project upcoming cash flow
4. Create quality, unique, trustworthy documents that address every client need
5. Ensure your documents meet all legal requirements, including state specific documents
6. Access information when you are away from the office
7. Secure and backup your data

MEET COUNSELPRO™

CounselPro8

The Academy's proprietary law firm management system, CounselPro™, provides a unified platform that integrates marketing, document production, accounting, and law firm management.

This powerful solution supports Academy recommended marketing procedures, allowing you to keep track of marketing activities, costs, seminar *"sweeps,"* events, results, and most importantly, the people. The ability to tie marketing efforts to individual clients allows for tracking of the client's lifetime value, showing the value of initial and repeat business.

Document production is built into CounselPro™, and provides all the available estate planning documents and opinions you will need. It is continuously reviewed by the Academy's education department to ensure it remains current. The final product is a uniquely designed, comprehensive document delivered in a standard word processing format.

Simple yet sophisticated reporting will help you manage your firm by showing the return of investment of your marketing efforts, the conversion rate on seminar attendees, and the closing rate of your personal consultations. You can view upcoming final signings or stalled files, which will allow you to effectively project and manage the firm's cash flow.

 Check out the Free Stuff section of this book for a link to a demonstration of this state-of-the-art software.

LAW FIRM WEBSITES, SEO AND SOCIAL MEDIA

If you aren't found online, you don't exist. These days you simply cannot cut corners on your web presence. Law firms must treat their website and social media activity as the marketing tool that it is.

Web content needs to be constantly updated. You need someone on your team who knows what they're doing to help you create the most powerful brand and to keep you ranked so you're easily found on search engines. The majority of Academy Members choose to use Academy Web and Social Media services (available as an option) because it is more effective to deal directly with a source that works only with your type of business.

Academy Members also have access to customizable websites for their firms. The WordPress platform allows you to take the driver's seat and tailor many features of your website without the need for HTML experience or knowledge. This easy-to-use new website control panel will allow your team to:

- Upload your own photos and logos
- Embed videos
- Customize your own sidebars on the fly
- Create new web pages with the click of a button
- Add social media and marketing plugins
- Change the color theme at anytime
- Update or add attorney and team member profiles
- Upload files to share with clients and friends of the firm
- Take advantage of the Academy's optional SEO and Social Media Program

---

WHAT MEMBERS HAVE TO SAY

"The quality is noticed by clients and colleagues alike, as I regularly receive compliments on the quality of the website. In this regard, the Academy focuses on two key issues for our firm's website:

(1) The website is easy for prospective clients to find, which gives the law firm a chance to be retained; and

(2) The website educates current and prospective clients, without a lot of the legalese, which is something that clients appreciate.

For me, I consider the Academy's services to be a no-brainer.

—Texas Member

SYSTEM 6—INTEGRATED MARKETING AND PUBLIC RELATIONS SYSTEM
Multiple Marketing Activities Generating an Endless Supply of Qualified Prospects

Don't put all your eggs in one basket.

You may be successful focusing on running ads and conducting public seminars—but in our experience, your luck with attendance will eventually run out or at least hit a bumpy road.

To establish a truly successful practice, your marketing plan (emphasizing the word "plan") needs to generate a variety of estate planning and elder law work from numerous sources.

This way, if one source dries up or there is a problem of some sort, your business is not in danger. There are basically five ways to increase your revenue:

1. Increase your fees
2. Provide existing clients with more services
3. Public marketing for new clients
4. Private marketing for new clients
5. Networking or referred new clients

Your marketing plan needs to include *detailed* steps that incorporate *all* of those sources.

The Marketing Systems available at the Academy include everything necessary for public and private seminar marketing as well as a rich cultivation of referrals—and don't forget the marketing tools necessary to stay in touch with clients and their family members, as well.

This too starts with a specific and detailed plan. The Academy updates a marketing planning template each year for the Membership and this plan template is also provided to VIP Guests attending any Boot Camp.

 The Academy also has a more detailed report on marketing your law firm. Feel free to contact us and ask that the eReport to be sent to you.

SYSTEM 7—NO STRESS CLIENT ENGAGEMENT SYSTEM
Predictably Inspiring Consumers to Take Action and Retain Your Firm

This is one of the most critical systems for success in the law firm and the success or failure of this system rests entirely on the attorney.

When you know you have 25 appointments on the calendar for next week and you also have confidence that the manner in which you conduct these meetings results consistently in 91% retention (or 85% or 89%), the math is a lot easier to do.

Many attorneys make the mistake of thinking their marketing isn't working when the problem is, the consultations that aren't working.

The number one area in which most attorneys need to improve? Stop talking so much.

There is a system for personal consultations. The system revolves around structuring the meeting properly. You don't actually want to answer the potential client's questions until you've asked all the questions you need them to answer first.

Another big trap in the consultation is that many attorneys allow the client to sit right down, pull out a yellow pad and start asking questions. Any attorney worth their salt will jump at the opportunity to answer correctly. Unfortunately for many, they go into more detail than the client needs to hear. The time the attorney spends talking is time the client didn't get to spend talking about what bothers them the most.

That's the system. Creating an environment where you help your clients get in touch with exactly what their concerns are. Not only is there a unique system for properly conducted consultations, but this system is centered around getting to the bottom of what's most important to the client.

This system aids in guiding that client through emotional topics with finesse and leading them to a decision that is in their own best interest—whether it's to proceed or not.

 There is an optional Academy *"coaching program"* for Member attorneys who want additional emphasis in this area. The Academy has developed a lot of resources to perfect this system. If you would like a more detailed report on this particular system, send us an email at <u>Questions@aaepa.com</u> and we'll be happy to provide it at no cost.

SYSTEM 8—EFFICIENT WORKFLOW SYSTEMS
Drafting, Reviewing, and Executing State-of-the-Art Estate Plans

What is the number of days between a personal consultation and a final signing ceremony in your firm and how hectic is all the preparation?

Once a client retains the law firm, the *"behind the scenes"* action should be smooth and enjoyable. Clients should be in awe of every little experience through this process. Too often, however, it's a nightmare.

One secret to smooth, efficient production goes back to technology. Your software has to be solid, easy to use and up-to-date.

 The Academy's CounselPro™ software is a full estate planning document assembly program connected under the same hood as the database that runs the firm. Check out the Academy Benefits at a Glance section of this book for a full list of the estate planning documents in CounselPro™ as well as the endless list of management reports and several hundred pre-written letters for prospects, clients, and the law firm's centers of influence.

Part of the workflow process focuses on the job descriptions and talents of your team. Aside from a Document Assembly and Funding expert, you will end up with a Final Signing Paralegal.

Sometimes it takes a little effort to see yourself delegating a Final Signing. Make sure you ask other Academy Members what their view is about this transition. It may surprise you!

SYSTEM 9—CONTINUING LEGAL EDUCATION SYSTEM
Staying on the Cutting Edge of Effective Legal Strategies

Again, whether you end up joining the Academy Membership or not, you must find a resource for staying on top of the changes in the law. Estate planning is notorious for constant law changes.

You must also have confidence in the quality of the legal documents you're using.

The Academy's legal education department consists of some of the finest legal minds in this field. The department's sole responsibility is the behind the scenes research and analysis to answer every question an attorney may have about any given case.

The attorneys in our legal education department are prepared to guide each Member through whatever learning curve the Member happens to have.

The support offered is provided only to the attorneys in a Member firm. It ranges from basic to advanced questions. Most questions are answered the same day.

Our attorneys are responsible for conducting monthly training calls, planning and presenting sessions and courses across the country, and are regularly published in relevant publications.

We also strive to offer regular updates on recent rulings, and constant document language reviews as well as routine reviews of all Academy marketing materials as laws change.

This team spends most hours researching, participating in their own study, and writing or interviewing for national publications.

Some Members justify Membership solely on their use and confidence in this resource.

SYSTEM 10—ANCILLARY BUSINESS SYSTEMS
Leveraging Client Relationships to Generate Multiple Sources of Revenue

Once the foundation of an estate planning or elder law practice is in place, it works beautifully to add services that are natural complements to your practice.

Have you ever considered adding an ancillary business to provide your clients with a higher level of service?

In recent years, many Academy Members have found that with proper disclosure, appropriate licenses, and systems for offering Financial Services, they can add a layer of confidence and service for clients. What could provide more assurance than for a client to have a financial plan that dovetails with his or her estate plan?

Clients like having their financial plan fit with their estate plan.

There are a variety of ways to set this type of business up and myriad ways of ensuring that the success of that business does not interrupt the success of your law firm.

It cannot be stressed enough, *the systems in your law firm should be solid before you launch a second business.* The timing of such a venture is essential, as are things like ensuring that the separation of files meets standards, knowing which licenses to study for, and maintaining accurate accounting for this business.

 Ask us for a list of Members who have successfully set financial services in motion in their area. There are rules in each state that you must be aware of as well as best practices for setting up a second business.

When done properly, this type of business is a win-win!

SYSTEM 11—ONGOING MASTERMIND SYSTEM
Structures to Participate in a Community of Like-Minded Attorneys

One of the most important benefits of Membership is the most difficult to describe. This is because attorneys who are not part of the Academy cannot generally conceive of a place where fellow estate planning attorneys will openly share what works, what hasn't worked, or collaborate on new document language or estate planning solutions.

At bar meetings you don't see that. You don't see it anywhere! Picture a room full of 150 attorneys with their financials in their pocket... all willing to pull those numbers out and either ask for input or provide some supportive words of wisdom. It's not always about the financials. Hallway conversations may revolve around, *"How is it that you set up your practice so you're closed on Friday? I've always wanted to do that!"*

Women attorneys gather to discuss their experiences as lawyers in this field. Attorneys under 40 connect as well as those with decades of experience to share. Many of the sessions at events are made up of panels of these esteemed estate planning attorneys sharing their experiences and their results.

 Be sure you ask Members about this aspect of Membership and how it has impacted their practice.

ACADEMY BOOT CAMPS

It all starts with Boot Camp. There is a reason the introduction to Academy Systems is called a Boot Camp. You go in acting and thinking one way—and in a matter of two days, you come out seeing the world, the practice, and your potential in a whole new light.

We invite qualified attorneys from around the country to attend our Boot Camps as VIP Guests. The Boot Camp consists of over 8 hours of training on the fundamentals to have or put in place before you can build your strong, successful practice.

We ask VIP Guests to be in a geographic area where we have an opening for Membership. They also need to qualify by meeting Membership requirements. Our VIPs submit a Membership application prior to attending the Boot Camp, even though they are clear that there is no requirement for them to join.

NOT EVERY APPLICANT IS ACCEPTED

We open our Boot Camps to VIP Guest attorneys in an effort to let them take a look behind our curtain and see everything there is to see, to meet Members and also for us to meet these VIP Guests. By the time the Boot Camp and Summit concludes, the VIP Guest knows if it feels like a fit, and we know if it feels like a good match, as well. Not every VIP Guest is accepted as a Member.

The tuition for this Boot Camp is equivalent to what an attorney could generate by retaining two estate plans. Be sure to ask us if we are currently offering a scholarship for an upcoming Boot Camp.

WHAT HAPPENS AT THE BOOT CAMP?

The Boot Camp is led by Academy founders Robert Armstrong and Sanford M. Fish, along with a few others on the Academy team. The group is intentionally small. Boot Camps are generally limited to 12-15 VIP Guest Law Firms along with up to 10 Member Firms (Members often come back to "reboot," bringing new team members of their firm).

Typically, a VIP Guest will attend with partners, spouses and/or key team members in their firm. The Boot Camps begin at 8:00am and go beyond dinner that same evening, starting again the next morning by 8:00am.

The Boot Camp is structured, well, a lot like a Boot Camp! It's not just that the agenda is packed, the agenda is filled with the kind of sessions that ignite something in the attendees. Ideas and plans start to come together and it becomes an experience that attendees will remember for the rest of their lives, whether or not they end up joining the Membership.

At the end of the Boot Camp, you will have a new way of seeing your opportunities in the area of planning, marketing, client retention, estate planning production workflow, client relations, hiring, management, and leadership.

It is truly an opportunity to step back and work "on" your business!

NIKKI NASSIRI manages the Academy Boot Camps and has all the latest details on any upcoming events. Email info@aaepa.com for dates or with any questions about whether you are eligible to attend.

BOOT CAMP AGENDA

The 11 Essential Systems™ are presented in detail. You already read additional information on these systems a little earlier in this book, but experiencing the systems rather than just reading about them is an entirely different story.

Here are the systems we review at the Boot Camp:

Creating a Purpose and Profit-Driven Practice with Academy Founders Robert Armstrong and Sanford M. Fisch

1. **Strategic Planning System:** Aligning Your Business with Your Personal Values
2. **Finance and Operations Management System:** Managing by the Numbers
3. **A Systems Approach to Leadership:** Creating a Firm Culture, Focusing on Unique Abilities and the Road to Mastery
4. **Staff Accountability and Team Building System:** Putting the Right People with the Right Skills in the Right Positions
5. **Comprehensive Technology System:** Leveraging Online and Offline Tools to Draft Documents and Manage Your Firm
6. **Integrated Marketing and Public Relations System:** Multiple Marketing Activities Generating an Endless Supply of Qualified Prospects
7. **No Stress Client Engagement System:** Predictably Inspiring Consumers to Take Action and Retain Your Firm

8. **Efficient Workflow System:** Drafting, Reviewing and Executing State-of-the-Art Estate Plans
9. **Continuing Legal Education System:** Staying on the Cutting Edge of Effective Legal Strategies
10. **Ancillary Business Systems:** Leveraging Client Relationships to Generate Multiple Sources of Revenue
11. **Ongoing Mastermind System:** Structures to Participate in a Community of Like-Minded Attorneys

Once the 11 Essential Systems™ are presented, participants roll up their sleeves and put the information to work. Another 3-4 hours is spent working with participants on how to put that information into action:

Creating Your Roadmap for Success
- Hands-On Marketing Plan Creation
- Identify revenue goals
- Identify possible marketing and promotional activities
- Calendar revenue generating and networking activities

 For an upcoming schedule of Boot Camps, refer to our website at http://www.aaepa.com/academy-events/

ACADEMY SUMMITS

The Academy conducts two Summits per year. Each Fall the Summit is in San Diego and each Spring the Summit is usually located in a city on the eastern half of the country. These events always start after a Boot Camp is completed. Boot Camp participants can simply come two days before the Summit for this additional personal training.

Summits always begin on a Thursday, promptly at 1:00pm and go through the following Sunday, ending at noon. Thursday is kicked off with our State of the Academy meeting, featuring a great keynote speaker as well as keynotes presented by the Academy founders.

The sessions for the remainder of the Summit include substantive legal topics ranging from VA and Medicaid Planning to basic and advanced estate planning. We have guest speakers on those topics as well as marketing topics, new programs are released and we host technology topics that keep our Members on the cutting edge. The Summit generally provides 10-14 hours of CLE for attendees. Summits are reserved only for Members and anyone on their team they invite to attend, along with a handful of invitation-only VIP Guests.

 For an upcoming schedule of Summit events, refer to our website at http://www.aaepa.com/academy-events/

DENNIS SANDOVAL, J.D., LL.M. (Tax), CELA, AEP, Director Emeritus
STEVE HARTNETT, J.D., LL.M., Director of Education

CLASSROOM CONFERENCE CALLS

The Academy offers Members a monthly webinar conducted by the Academy Education Department. The topics covered may relate to changes in the law, updates in the Academy documents or case studies.

Members have the opportunity to participate on those webinars live or to refer to the recordings at a later date.

It is not uncommon for a new Academy Member to consult with the Education Department and put together a curriculum of webinars that fits the estate planning experience and technical goals the new Member wants to achieve.

As you can imagine, the legal team at the Academy plays a major teaching role at our Summits where they are also available for private consultations throughout the event.

Over the years, the team has put together what we call Core Curriculum I and II. These intense programs are done at your own pace and cover the very basics in estate planning to the most *complex* issues.

 We offer a number of technical sessions either from these webinars or from Summit sessions. Be sure to let us know what type of topic you are interested in reviewing and we'll make sure to get a recording sent to you. Simply email us at questions@aaepa.com to let us know what topics interest you.

SUSAN RUSSEL
Director of Member Services

PRACTICE BUILDING COACHING AND WEBINARS

Our Member Services Team conducts regular phone meetings with attorneys in the Membership. These coaching calls consist of an agenda that the Practice Building Coach and the attorney establish when the goals of the attorney are laid out.

Occasionally, Members ask their team to participate on some of the topics covered on those coaching calls. These calls aren't just "new ideas" and "try this" conversations, these calls are hard-hitting accountability calls. You aren't able to boost your firm's success without towing the line. If you tend to get distracted by shiny objects or perhaps you suffer from analysis paralysis, your coach will shine a light on those things so you have a chance to see what might be getting in the way of progress.

The Member Services team also presents monthly webinars on Leadership, Management, Marketing, and Planning. Like our Legal Education webinars, these are recorded and available to Members or their teams any time they want to review them.

The goal with these webinars is to take a module that Members have in their Practice Building Handbook, or Integrated Marketing Guide and walk the Member or their team step-by-step through execution.

CounselPro 8

SOFTWARE TRAINING WEBINARS

The Academy's Software Support Department offers live, interactive webinars on a monthly basis. Most of these webinars focus on a specific use of the software. For example, one session may go into detail on how to create a mail merge, another webinar may focus on creating management reports reflecting the status of every open file in the firm.

All of the webinars are recorded and can be accessed on the Academy's eLearning site.

At least once per year, Members are asked to bring laptops to an Academy Summit for hands-on training. This training is typically so interactive that it is not recorded.

RITA CHAIRES
Director of Web Services

WEBSITE AND ONLINE MARKETING TRAINING WEBINARS

The internet is now part of how we live our everyday lives, from Facebooking to conducting a Google search. Attorneys need to have a stellar web presence in order to stay competitive. Over 90% of Academy Members have a website built by our team of expert designers, developers, and marketers. These websites are built on the WordPress platform, which allows Members to customize many features without the need for HTML experience or knowledge. All websites also include an email marketing component, such as MailChimp or Constant Contact.

Extensive tutorials on the use and customization of WordPress and MailChimp are available on the Academy's eLearning site and the Web team is always available for one-on-one training. The Academy's Online Marketing Group (OMG) presents a monthly webinar providing training on various topics that range from websites and SEO to social media and other important aspects of online marketing. These webinars are also recorded and available on our eLearning site.

ACADEMY ROOTS

In 1993, the Academy only focused on estate planning law firm marketing and workflow systems. Since that time tools and coaching have evolved to become the most comprehensive support available in the country.

Academy Membership benefits cover every component of a law firm. It is difficult to list each benefit. Most Members simply cannot implement each one. We have tried to list the benefits that Members rely on the most here. If you have questions about the details on any listed benefit, do not hesitate to email us at **questions@aaepa.com**.

NEW MEMBER SUPPORT, TOOLS AND COACHING

One of the most important benefits at the beginning of Membership is the assignment of a Practice Building Coach.

The role the Practice Building Coach (PBC) plays for a new Member makes all the difference to their Membership. From day one of Membership, the PBC schedules a call and helps the new Member unpack the tools and become familiar with what the next steps will be.

The PBC lays out the "New Member Implementation Plan" with each new law firm owner. This is basically a schedule that adds some structure to the implementation of the tools that line up with the attorney's vision.

TOOLS FOR LAUNCHING

- Executive starter kit including manuals and recordings of training
- Access to Members-Only website and all available software, PowerPoint, Word or recorded resources
- Access to Member listserv
- Software installation & support coach
- Start-up image building tools
- Tools/forms/instruction to obtain efficient workflow
- Strategic planning template and organizational chart
- Marketing planning calendar customization support
- Customized seminar presentation tools and training
- Personal consultation training
- Video and written training information on CounselPro™ software

- Academy implementation training for law firm team members
- A host of endorsed vendors offering services or special fees to Members
  - NGL: Funeral Trust Company
  - DocuBank
  - Send Out Cards
  - Mozy Pro Online Backup Services
  - Credit Card Processing Vendor
  - ADP
  - Office Depot

PRACTICE BUILDING SUPPORT

One-on-one coaching with unique agenda for regular meeting tied to:

- Strategic planning process and discussion
- Marketing plan, execution and review
- Leadership and management of the law practice, financials and staffing
- Accountability

Personnel systems

- Hiring module including advertising copy, job descriptions, orientation schedules and offer letters along with sample employment contracts
- Testing recommendations and benchmarks for hiring
- Customizable employee handbook

Access to Academy Members-Only website
- Access to all archives of past courses covering all areas of the practice (audio recordings and materials), well over 20,000 web pages of coursework and resource material

Practice management systems:
- Planning and organizational set-up
- Creating a client-base
- Workflow systems for document creation and final signings
- Practice building audio recording series in the starter kit

Regular and optional training on personal consultations

Business planning support
- Strategic planning forms and coaching
- Marketing planning / coaching calls
- Financial analysis with access to comparison to other Member firms
- Practice building coaching and follow up tracking support

Regular Membership marketing and practice building webinars

MARKETING AND PUBLIC RELATIONS

Integrated Marketing Guide

- Detailed training modules for law firm team members on how to execute all Academy marketing programs

Marketing Calendar Template and Coaching

- Each year a draft for a law firm marketing calendar is released for law firm use. Coaching and training sessions on this topic are strong

Ad and Direct Mail Library

- Coaching support aids in customization of ads and direct mail
- Academy designer available for existing or special marketing pieces

Niche Marketing Modules and Presentation Tools

(Seminars include unique advertising, direct mail copy, seminar handouts, and customizable powerpoint slides and script)

- LGBT marketing tools and seminar
- Farmer / Rancher marketing and seminar
- Business owner marketing and seminar
- Legacy Wealth Planning marketing and seminars
- Marketing tools to care for your existing clients
- CE and CLE courses available for specific audiences

Referral Marketing Seminars and Tools

- Online eAlerts and instruction provided
- Optional eAlert delivery system

- Optional Send Out Cards program with special custom designs for each use

40+ Reports Available for Consumers
- For use in eAlert or online offers as well as in your lobby or at seminars on specific estate planning and elder law related topics

Optional Medicaid Marketing System
- The Academy has special pricing arranged for Medicaid marketing training and support.

Seminar Direct Mail System
- Not only are all of these seminar related letters written, they are loaded into the software. There is also a training module detailing the step-by-step execution for maximum response.

Endorsed Seminar Marketing Guide
- This guide walks a Marketing Coordinator through steps ranging from introduction to organization through invitation and presentation

Marketing Through Non-Profits Guide

Email Content and Instruction for Building Referral Relationships

Optional Personal Consultation or Recordings of Past Trainings

Monthly Estate Planning Articles

Image Building Tools

- Quarterly consumer newsletters; in print and on Member websites
- Law firm brochures
- Over 15 press release templates

Working with TV and Radio Module

Working with the Media Guide

Online Press Release Presence for Law Firm Successes and for Noteworthy Accomplishments

Specific Marketing Seminars or Programs Provided with Membership

(Seminar Systems include marketing materials, seminar hand-out, slides and script)

- Legacy Wealth Planning Seminar, System for Those With a Living Trust
- Legacy Wealth Planning Seminar, System for the General Public
- Legacy Wealth Planning Seminar, System for Your Own Client Base
- Basic Estate Planning Seminar System
- Asset Protection Seminar System
- Medicaid Planning Seminar System
- IRA Consumer Seminar System
- Estate Planning for the Farmer/ Rancher/Land Owner
- Special Needs Seminar System

- Famous Estates Audience Warm-Up Slides and Videos
- LGBT Estate Planning Seminar System
- 12-Part CE Program for Advisors
- IRA Planning CE Course for Advisors
- Family Business Succession Planning CE Course for Advisors
- Total Return Unitrust CE Course
- Customized Quarterly Newsletters*
- Co-Author Book Projects for Members*
- Proprietary Client Presentation Binders, Tabs to Match the Software*
- My Legacy Wealth Planning Workbooks for Consumers

COUNSELPRO™ DOCUMENTS

CounselPro™ is an Academy proprietary solution that has been structured to support each Academy system. CounselPro™ is a cloud-based solution, which makes it accessible anywhere the internet is available on PCs, Macs, tablets and mobile devices. All server updates, patches, security, and backups are included (provided by ActionStep). No special hardware or software is required (Microsoft Word is required to view and edit documents after creation).

Estate Planning documents are created directly within Counsel-Pro™. Powered by the cloud based version of HotDocs, a simple question and answer scenario determines which questions need to be answered to create an estate plan. Produced documents are stored within CounselPro™, so no backup is required. Members may also choose to download the documents to their local system.

Revocable Living Trust
- Joint Revocable Living Trust and Restatement
- Married Separate Revocable Living Trust and Restatement
- Unmarried Revocable Living Trust and Restatement
- Simple Married Joint Revocable Living Trust and Restatement
- Simple Married Separate Revocable Living Trust and Restatement

Legacy Wealth Trusts
- Joint Legacy Wealth Trust and Restatement
- Married Separate Legacy Wealth Trust and Restatement
- Unmarried Legacy Wealth Trust and Restatement
- Simple Married Joint Legacy Wealth Trust and Restatement
- Simple Married Separate Legacy Wealth Trust and Restatement

Other Trusts
- Family Retirement Preservation Trust—Irrevocable as well as Revocable
- Qualified Personal Residence Trust
- Intervivos QTIP

Wills
- A/B Testamentary Will
- Married Intermediate Will

- Unmarried Intermediate Will
- Simple Married Will
- Unmarried Simple Will

Supplemental Needs Trusts
- Revocable Supplemental Needs Trust
- Irrevocable Supplemental Needs Trust
- (d)(4)(A) Medicaid Payback Trust
- (c)(2)(B)(iv) Medicaid
- Qualification Trust
- 76-270 Special Needs Trust

ILITS
- Married Joint Irrevocable Life Insurance Trust
- Married Separate Irrevocable Life Insurance Trust
- Unmarried Irrevocable Life Insurance Trust

Medicaid
- Family Income Trust (Married Joint, Married Separate, and Unmarried)
- Family Discretionary Trust (Married Joint, Married Separate, and Unmarried)
- Family Gifting Trust (Married Joint, Married Separate, and Unmarried)

Advanced Estate Planning Documents
- Standard Charitable Remainder Annuity Trust
- Net Income Charitable Remainder Annuity Trust
- Net Income with Make-up Charitable Remainder Annuity Trust

- Standard Charitable Remainder Unitrust
- Net Income Charitable Remainder Unitrust
- Net Income with Make Up Charitable Remainder Unitrust
- Charitable Remainder Unitrust

Other Trusts
- Private Annuity Trust
- Family and Spouse Gifting Trust
- Grantor Retained Income Trust
- Grantor Retained Annuity Trust
- Grantor Retained Unitrust
- Charitable Remainder Trust (10 varieties)
- Charitable Lead Annuity Trust
- Charitable Lead Unitrust

Other Documents
- Self-Cancelling Installment Note
- Family Limited Liability Company (IRC2036 and Simple)
- Family Limited Partnership (IRC2036 and Simple)

Ancillary and State Specific Docs—for all 50 states
- Notary Acknowledgements
- Pour-Over Will
- Property Agreements (Community Property/Tenants in Common Property)
- Power of Attorney for Property
- Statutory Durable Power of Attorney for Health Care
- Statutory Living Will/Physicians Directive
- HIPAA Authorization

Proprietary Processing for:
- Commonwealths
- County/Parish/Judicial Districts/ County Absenteeism
- Statutory Homesteads

COUNSELPRO™ DATABASE

A completely customized version of ActionStep software. The software has been structured to support each Academy System. We highly recommend viewing the CounselPro™ demo at **www.aaepa.com/software**. The Academy Tech Support team coordinates the conversion from a Member's existing database to CounselPro™ and sets up their customized database at the beginning of Membership.

The database side of CounselPro™ consists of:

- Firm management database loaded with over 300 letters
- Customized workflows to keep law firm team members from missing any critical steps
- Countless workflow management reports
- Personal installation and setup
- One-on-one software training
- Unlimited access to software tech support
- Software training video and audio sessions
- Regular software training webinars and/or conference calls
- Online backup system recommendations and vendor

LAW FIRM WEBSITES

Custom Law Firm Websites*

- Hosted and fully maintained by Academy
- Contemporary, mobile-responsive designs built on the WordPress platform
- Integrated contact management and email marketing system
- Easily customizable by law firms
- Tracking and reporting of site activity, including leads received
- Optional hosted law firm email

Optional Online Marketing Support

- Three levels of service to meet the needs of every Member
- Content marketing, including blogs, videos and infographics
- SEO services, including back linking, directory placement, video marketing, and seminar promotions
- Social media marketing
- One-on-one coaching/training

Extensive Members-Only Website and eLearning Platform

- 24/7 access to over 20,000 pages of coursework and resource material
- Hours of recorded training modules
- Member Shared Items for use in your own practice
- Online shop-site offering discounted supplies
- Active listserv and forums for Members and staff

CLE AND LEGAL SUPPORT

- Academy CLE requirement of 36 hours is noted on Member listing
- "Fellow" designation available to recognize higher level of experience among Members, annotated on Member listing as well as Members' bio
- Substantive training
- Basic and advanced educational events
- Optional tax, elder law, IRA or other estate planning related courses
- One-on-one legal support, email or phone answers to specific legal questions
- Member guides on substantive issues
- Substantive law training library
- Member alerts on current developments
- Basic estate planning course
- Updates on recent rulings
- Focused advanced case design training
- Practical drafting training
- Monthly educational conference calls
- Frequently asked questions
- Document language committee made up of cross-section of the membership

- Monthly educational conference calls/webinars
- Courses on advanced topics
- Regular document and marketing materials updates
- Core curriculum I recording and materials
- Core curriculum II recording and materials*
- Core curriculum III recording and materials*
- Recordings of past guest speakers and topics

MORE MEMBER BENEFITS

- Geographic exclusivity
- Right to promote academy affiliation
- Access to all academy products
- Transferable Membership*
- Volume discounts on vendors services and supplies
- Member networking
- Members-only meetings
- Members and staff listservs
- Participation in financial database
- Participation in national deed filing service
- Model chart of accounts
- Peak Performers Program*
- Consultation Mastery Program*
- Medicaid Program*
- Speaker SchooL*
- Two legal Summit events per year
- Optional advanced topic is typically offered at Fall Summits in San Diego
  - Hands-on computer breakout training at most Fall Summits in San Diego
  - Marketing focus at most Spring Summit breakout sessions

FINANCIAL SERVICES SUPPORT

- Financial and Insurance organizations including financial services coaching expertise
- Guidance on getting licensed
- Consultation on setting up a financial services company
- Various necessary sample forms such as appropriate disclosure
- Emphasis on Comprehensive Wealth Care for clients
- Analysis of law firm and financial services financials with coaching on setting goals and improving results

* Available at extra cost

IT'S ALL "MOST IMPORTANT" AT ONE TIME OR ANOTHER

SAUL KOBRICK
Garden City, NY
Member Since 1996

"Why is the Academy important to me, or what do I most like about it? I really thought about it. The first thing that came to mind, for me, was

the living trust seminar. That, to me, was the most important thing when I first joined because that was the way I was able to get clients.

But then, we started to get clients and I realized we had to do documents. So then, the document assembly program became extremely important. And then, of course, there were all these legal questions.

And Dennis and Steve have really been fantastic with the education department, responsive, quick. You know we need answers quickly, and pretty much they're usually on the spot.

Also, everyone talks about the collegiality of this group. I think that all emanates from us continually coming to these meetings. You see the same faces, and hopefully a lot of new faces continually. But there's a real group effort or group feeling in this Academy.

I think that also translates, that in my office, I feel like I belong truly to a national law firm. Because I remember the other day we had some probate we needed to be done. I think it was in North Carolina. I was able to speak to Cheryl David and get that taken care of. When I need a deed in Florida I call up Robert Kulas, and he's able to take care of the deeds for me. I do deeds in New York for many other Members. I don't think there's any organization like that any place. I'm really glad to be a part of it."

—Saul Kobrick, New York

WEBINAR INVITATION FOR ATTORNEYS

Be Our Guest, Register at **www.aaepa.com/5Strat**
Or Call 800.846.1555

On our *5 Proven Strategies to Boost Your Profits & the Top 3 Mistakes that Can Put Your Practice in a Tail Spin* webinar, you'll hear the Academy founders review important points you can implement after the webinar.

Compiling over 20 years of proven business building resources, Robert Armstrong and Sanford M. Fisch are extracting the *Best of the Best* techniques and giving you the essential tools you need to start creating your own version of the perfect law practice!

Success can boil down to 5 things you do and 3 things you don't do. Those 5 things are easy to do—they're also easy **not** to do. The same is true in any part of our lives. You have a wonderful opportunity to tune in and hear two experienced estate planning attorneys and entrepreneurs, share openly, what they've learned and what they teach. You can learn first-hand how to build a profitable and efficient law practice—the practice you've been dreaming of since law school!

Product	Where to Order	When to Order	Purpose	Estimated Price
Marketing Planning Calendar	Online Download	ASAP (1st day of membership)	Planning & Marketing	Included
Strategic Planning Worksheet	Online Download	ASAP (1st day)	Planning & Marketing	Included
Implementation Checklist	Online Download	ASAP (1st day)	Implementation	Included
Seminar Ad, Direct Mail Letter and Postcard	Order through PBC*	ASAP (allow 3 weeks for delivery)	Marketing & PR	Included
Legacy Wealth Planning Myths Slide Show	Online Download	8 weeks before seminar	Presentations	Included
Legacy Wealth Planning Handouts (250)	Order with local printer	4 weeks before seminar	Presentations	Call local printers for quotes
My Legacy Workbook	Print Locally	2 weeks before seminar	Documents & Seminars	Call local printers for quotes
Academy Reports	Online Download	4 weeks before use	Public Relations	Included
Evaluation Forms	Online Download	4 weeks before seminar	Presentations	Included
Certificate & Map	Online Download	4 weeks before seminar	Presentations	Included

Product	Where to Order	When to Order	Purpose	Estimated Price
2 Boxes 2" LWP Binders and Tabs	Online Order (Academy Shop Site)	4 weeks before seminar	Documents	$350
Portfolio CDs Pre-recorded "Masters"	Online Order (Member duplicates in-house or use vendors)	4 weeks before use	Documents	$225 (plus cost for copies)
Portfolio Audio Recordings	Scripts Online (Member records at local studio)	8 weeks before use	Documents	Call local studios for quotes
Portfolio CD Duplication	In-house or local CD Duplication Company	4 weeks before seminar	Documents	$75 - $215
Client Intake Forms	Online Download or in CounselPro™	3 weeks before seminar	Documents	Included
Client Asset Books	Online Download	3 weeks before seminar	Documents	Included
Color Coded Plastic Sleeves	Century Business Solutions www.centurybusinesssolutions.com 800-767-0777	2 weeks before seminar	Documents (routing)	$1.46 each (Item # PW014)
Clear Plastic Folders	Century Business Solutions www.centurybusinesssolutions.com 800-767-0777	2 weeks before seminar	Documents (Originals)	$2.63 each (Item # EN00100PK)

Equipment Needed				
Product	**Where to Order**	**When to Order**	**Purpose**	**Estimated Price**
See *"Computer System Requirements"* List	In Starter Kit	ASAP	Practice Management	Call vendors for quotes
LCD Projector	Vendor information in Starter Kit	ASAP	Presentations	$2,000 - $3,200
Microphone	Radio Shack	ASAP	Presentations	$150 - $200
DocuBank	Enroll online at www.DocuBank.com	4 weeks before use	Documents	Per person rates $16 for 1 year $38 for 3 years $50 for 5 years
Seminar Screen	Local vendor	ASAP	Presentations	$300 - $600
Laptop (unless LCD runs on a *"chip"* containing the PowerPoint files)	Local vendor	ASAP	Presentations	$1,000 - $3,000
Office Supplies (paper, pencils, etc.)	Office Depot	ASAP	Practice Management	Call for quotes
Digital Voice Mail— Equipment or Local VM Service	Local vendor	ASAP	Practice Management	Call for quotes

	Additional Investments to Consider			
Product	**Where to Order**	**When to Order**	**Purpose**	**Estimated Price**
Law Firm Website	Online Order	4 weeks before use	Marketing & PR	$1850 setup $140/month
Search Engine Optimization and Social Media Program	Online Order	After website order	Marketing & PR	$2,625 - $2,850 setup $1,137 - $1,637/ month
Professional Profiles (500)	Order through PBC	4 weeks before use	Public Relations	Call for quote
Law Firm Brochures (500)	Order through PBC	4 weeks before use	Public Relations	Call for quote
Stationery	Local vendor	4 weeks before use	Marketing & PR	Call for quote
Consumer Newsletters (250)	Online Order	Quarterly	Marketing & PR	$199 plus shipping
CE Instructor Status	Order through PBC	2 months before use	Networking— offer Academy CE courses to CPAs, Advisors, etc.	Varies by State
Replacement Event & AAEPA Binders	Online Order or Download	When Needed	Practice Management	$85 each
Core Curriculum III Audio and Materials	Online Order	2 weeks before use	Education— Intermediate to Advanced Substantive Training Courses	$275
Summit Attendance (1 free seat)	Online Registration	Per Year	Education	Approx. $455 per add'l seat

Additional Investments to Consider				
Product	**Where to Order**	**When to Order**	**Purpose**	**Estimated Price**
Training Day (Optional)	Online Registration	Usually Twice Yearly	Education—follows most Summits on topics like 706 prep, Initial Consult Training, Medicaid, etc.	Approx. $325 - $800 per seat
Year-Long Initial Consultation Coaching Program	Online Order (Highly Recommended)	4 weeks before use	Initial Consultations	Annual Fee
MPS Elder Law Program	Online Download	4 weeks before use	Marketing & PR	$2,797 Upfront $400/Mo.
Scanner/ Copier	Local Vendors	When going paperless	Practice Management	Call vendors for quotes
MozyPro	Order Online	ASAP	Computer Back up	$6.95/Mo. per server $3.95/Mo. per desktop computer plus $.50/GB
QuickBooks	www.quickbooks.com	ASAP	Accounting	$250 - $500

We encourage all attorneys who are considering attending a Boot Camp, Summit or preparing to join the Membership to speak with at least three Members. The best Members to speak with are often attorneys who have a background similar to yours.

- If you're leaving a large firm, ask us for the names of Members who have been in that position.
- If you're transitioning from litigation or any other specific field, ask for Members with that experience.

- Perhaps you are a CPA or from a small marketplace or you focus almost entirely on a niche inside of a market... we can introduce you to Members who have that in common.
- If you are planning to retire and you want to set things up so they are easier to transition, we have Members with that experience.
- If you have estate planning experience and you want to talk to an attorney who has taken their practice from one level to another, or perhaps structured their practice so they only work 3 or 4 days per week, let us know.

Tell us what position you're in now and what your goals are for your practice and your life and we are happy to put you in touch with as many Members as you would like to speak with.

Membership is not for everyone. Doing a little due diligence can really put your mind at ease.

Email info@aaepa.com for a referral to a Member that fits the description you want on the phone! Then ask them anything you want. Ask Members about:

- Their start up experience
- Revenue they tracked
- Academy systems they use and don't use
- Academy CounselPro™ software
- Marketing strategies and tools
- The quality of the coaching

- The legal education and requirements
- Whatever you have on your mind

 You can help yourself to our online Membership Directory found at http://www.aaepa.com/member_directory/ or describe the background of the attorney you would like to connect with, and we can give you a hand.

BAR AND CREDIT STANDING

The first step toward Academy Membership is the submission of an application. The approval process for this application typically takes a week.

As part of the application process, we talk to professional references, contact the bar for each state in which the applicant is licensed to practice, and perform a full credit check.

REQUIRED RESOURCES

After an attorney's application is approved, we have a detailed conversation about the resources required to shift a practice into functioning at the level of an Academy Member firm.

Don't be shy about asking for common expenses that you may experience in your practice. Of course, those numbers depend on the team and the game plan you currently have and the speed with which you plan on transitioning to the tools and systems available at the Academy.

GEOGRAPHIC EXCLUSIVITY

Each Member signs an agreement that assures the Academy will not make Academy materials, tools, systems, coaching or Legal Education available to more than a specific number of attorneys in any given geographic area.

The geographic area typically revolves around population in contiguous counties. The number of Members allowed in any given metropolitan area is also impacted by the media in that area.

Members love this.

Because they don't have to worry about competing with one another, Academy Members enjoy an especially collaborative relationship—in fact, this is one of the main benefits of Membership. It is not uncommon for Academy attorneys to share their financial or marketing strategies or results openly with other Members.

CONTINUED LEGAL EDUCATION REQUIREMENT

Upon joining the Academy, Members gain a vast amount of estate planning experience in short order—regardless of their experience level when they started.

The Academy requires 36 annual hours of CLE in the areas of Estate Planning, Elder Law, Probate or Trust Administration. We make it easy to meet this requirement by offering legal education via monthly webinars, calls, and events.

BE COACHABLE

One of the hallmarks of Academy Members is that they're coachable. We liken this to a high-level athlete. There aren't any Michael Jordan's out there who don't have coaches they count on.

Being coachable is key.

"I've been a Member of the Academy, what they call I guess a 'founding Member' since June of 1993. The Academy never ceases to amaze me at the depth of new ideas, new techniques, new strategies that they come up with, always enabling us to improve ourselves, giving us the chance to do so and the support that's there.

I don't think there's any other organization in the country that offers the collegiality, the depth of resources, the diversity and the support that Academy Membership offers."

—Ohio Member

We have found, over the years, that the best way to show attorneys what we have and how the support works is to actually let them sample as much as possible. We invite you to help yourself to a long list of tools and webinars.

The easiest way to access all the free tools and education that we offer non-Members is to visit **www.aaepa. com/FreeStuff**. On that web page you will find links to the following tools and coursework attorneys find most useful.

ACADEMY BLOG

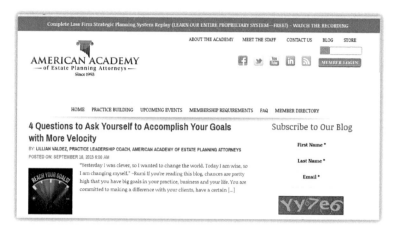

www.aaepa.com/blog

The Academy publishes a blog three times per week, like clockwork. It's entirely free and any attorney in an open or closed territory is welcome to subscribe. These blogs often feature:

- Law change information
- Substantive legal tips for estate planning or elder law firms
- Practice building recommendations
- Articles on leadership and management
- Messages from the founders
- Posts from Guest Bloggers

By going to **www.aaepa.com/blog**, and entering just your email address and name, we can deliver the blog to your inbox.

ACADEMY FACEBOOK FAN PAGE

https://www.facebook.com/
AmericanAcademyOfEstatePlanningAttorneys

Just like our blog, "liking" our Facebook Page is completely free and loaded with great stuff. We encourage attorneys to provide feedback on articles we post there as well as to submit suggestions on what else they would like to see. We try to repost interesting articles that tie to estate or financial planning so Academy Members and our attorney fans can repost them on their own fan pages. It makes it a lot easier for you to keep your own page interesting.

ACADEMY EVENTS
http://www.aaepa.com/academy-events/

If you are in a geographic area where we need a Member, and if you qualify to be a Member, we often invite attorneys to join us for Boot Camp and Summit events! You'll find the dates and locations of upcoming events on this page.

 If you'd like to have more of an idea on how the Boot Camp and Summits work, who should attend and who should not, along with more details about precisely what is covered at these events, please spend about 50 minutes going through our *"All About That Boot Camp"* Webinar. Register for this webinar by going to training.aaepa.com/bootcamp.

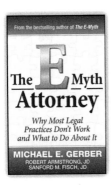

The E-Myth Attorney, Why Most Legal Practices Don't Work and What to Do About It, written by Michael E. Gerber, Robert Armstrong and Sanford M. Fisch

We can't give away all our materials for free, but this one is available on Amazon for about $18 and if you haven't read it— it is highly recommended. It even comes in audiobook form.

Book Description:
This book is the complete guide to the business of running a successful legal practice.

Many attorneys in small and mid-size practices are experts on the law, but may not have considered their practice from a business perspective.

The E-Myth Attorney fills this void, giving you powerful advice on everything you need to run your practice as a successful business, allowing you to achieve your goals and grow your practice. Featuring Gerber's signature easy-to-understand, easy-to-implement style, *The E-Myth Attorney* features:

- A complete start-up guide you can use to get your practice off the ground quickly, as well as comprehensive action steps for maximizing the performance of an existing practice
- Industry specific advice from two recognized legal experts who have developed a highly successful legal practice using Gerber's principles
- Gerber's universal appeal as a recognized expert on small businesses who has coached, taught, and trained over 60,000 small businesses

The E-Myth Attorney is the last guide you'll ever need to make the difference in building or developing your successful legal practice.

Required Reading for Small Law Firms & Sole Practitioners.

"As a young briefing attorney, a U.S. District Court judge once told me that there is more to the practice of law than being a good attorney. An abundance of knowledge and ability mean little if an attorney lacks the ability to lead his clients, associates, and staff. The attorney's knowledge also means little if the attorney lacks the ability to manage the equalizer that favors none, which is time. Therefore, in light of those challenges, if you seek an enlightened way to transform your law practice into a successful business that delivers quality legal services, and which is then transformed further into a successful enterprise that functions smoothly in your occasional absence, then you should read and heed the wisdom contained in The E-Myth Attorney. If you care not, then you risk repeating the failures of so many who came before you."

The Entrepreneurial Lawyer: A Guide to Creating a Thriving Law Firm and a Satisfying Life, **by Robert Armstrong and Sanford M. Fisch**

We are happy to provide you with a free version of this book in eBook form. You can request this book by emailing us at **questions@aaepa.com** and letting us know you'd like the eBook version.

If you would prefer to have a hard copy of the book, we offer them for sale on our website for $9.95 at **http://www.aaepa. com/academy-store/.**

Book Description:

Running a successful law practice means wearing two hats. Your clients are counting on you to be an expert in your area of law. At the same time, you have all the demands of running a small business—something many of us didn't fully anticipate when we graduated from law school.

Our legal education gave us the foundation we needed to become excellent legal practitioners, but few of us have the training necessary to build a successful business. The result is that we work as hard as we can to do excellent legal work, and we wonder why that doesn't result in a growing, thriving legal enterprise. So, we spend more time at the office being the best lawyers we can be, until our family and personal lives suffer and we start to lose our passion for the law.

The truth is, you can create a legal business that is not only growing but is highly profitable, and you can do it while taking time to enjoy life outside the office. The American Academy of Estate Planning Attorneys figured out how to do it more than two decades ago. Since then, we've helped hundreds of attorneys nationwide to transform their practices and their lives.

Our secret is simple. Systems.

FREE REPORTS AND WEBINARS

Numbers Don't Lie: Interpreting Your Law Firm Financials

This is a very informative report revealing the financial benchmarks that reflect a healthy practice. If you aren't keeping 40% of the gross revenue in your practice there are easy ways to find out where it is going and how to make the adjustments you need to make.

The Academy points out approximately 12 key benchmarks to keep an eye on. This report is free. The report is used as a handout for the Financial Benchmarks Webinar.

If you'd like a copy of this report, email us at **questions@aaepa. com** to request your free downloadable copy.

Financial Benchmarks Webinar (Replay)

45 Minutes with Jennifer Price reviewing a set of law firm financials. By the time the webinar is over, you'll have at least a dozen new ideas on how to look at your financials.

This is not an accounting class. This is a session intended to be used to immediately increase your revenue. You will identify how to set your fees, what percentage of your gross should be devoted to marketing, how many clients those marketing dollars should be generating and how to fix the numbers that don't seem to be stacking up. Materials included.

To request a replay, email **questions@aaepa.com** and ask for approval to access.

CounselPro™ 8

Introduction to how Academy software works as a CRM and document production program for the law firm.

CounselPro™ 8 offers a cloud based web application for Mac or PC. No need to worry about backups, upgrades, or expensive servers. This software is a database and document assembly program all in one and was built around the Academy's processes and systems.

During this demo you will get to see the actual software, get a glimpse of the legal documents and have a real feel for the ease of use.

There are no materials for this software demo.

To register, simply fill out the registration form at **www.aaepa. com/software** for immediate access.

STRATEGIC PLANNING WEBINAR

This is a MUST SEE webinar. It doesn't even matter if you're interested in Membership.

This webinar goes into detail on the Academy's first of 11 Systems. There is nothing sexy about having to draft a strategic plan for your firm, but the conversation is active and gets right to the heart of the fact that most unsuccessful attorneys DON'T plan, most successful attorneys DO... and details how that process works.

Presented by Robert Armstrong, Sanford M. Fisch and Jennifer Price. Materials are a big part of this webinar. You'll get the exact same forms that Academy Members use in their planning!

Don't forget to register for this one! Register by going to <u>training.aaepa.com/planningwebinar</u>.

"ALL ABOUT THAT BOOT CAMP" WEBINAR

If you can only watch two webinars, make this one of them. By the time you finish this 50 minute Webinar, you will have a clear view of who the Academy is and what you can gain from getting to know us better.

This webinar is facilitated by longtime Academy Member, attorney Jack Alpern. Robert Armstrong and Sanford Fisch speak a little on how they format our Boot Camps and what they strive to achieve. There are also guest Members present on this webinar who have a few words of wisdom to share.

This webinar is well worth your time. There are no materials, so all you need to do is register by going to **training.aaepa. com/bootcamp**.

E-MYTH ATTORNEY SPECIAL REPORT

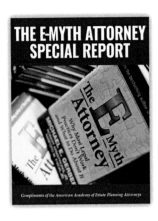

We've created a short report that highlights the most notable tips from the E-Myth Attorney Book. Get your free copy of this downloadable report by emailing us at **questions@aaepa.com**.

11 ESSENTIAL SYSTEMS: INDIVIDUAL REPORTS

We have written a 5-6 page report on each of the 11 Systems. If you're interested in learning more about a few systems at a time, this is the way to go. All 11 reports are available to download for free at **www.aaepa.com/11-essential-systems-report/**.

FULL SPECTRUM ESTATE PLANNER REPORT

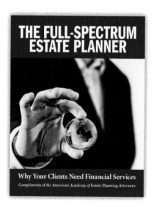

This report details the benefit to offering financial services as an option to your clients and some tips for integrating this ancillary business into your established estate planning firm.

Request your free copy of this report by emailing us at **questions@aaepa.com**.

ONLINE BOOT CAMP DELIVERED TO YOUR EMAIL

11 Steps to Building a Profitable, Systematized and Fulfilling Estate Planning Practice

Request our 11-day boot camp to uncover the time-tested lessons and processes American Academy members have used for over 25 years to transform their law firms into more efficient, effective and profitable business ventures. Once requested, you'll receive for the next 11 days a comprehensive training right to your inbox. Each training is full of concrete strategies and actionable steps that you can use immediately to experience more wealth, success, growth and fulfillment in your legal practice. Request it for free at **training.aaepa.com/11daybootcamp/**.

FREE COURSES: HELP YOURSELF!

Over the years, the Academy has featured an impressive number of speakers at events or on webinars as well as created courses for Members and Non-Members.

We have put together mini-courses that feature a compilation of our "Greatest Hits" that cover topics like:

- Strategic Planning
- Personal Consultation Training
- Asset Protection (a substantive session)
- Generating Referrals
- Top Estate Planning Questions Asked by Attorneys
- The Importance of Systems
- Integrating Your Marketing
- Search Engine Optimization for Law Firms
- and more!

We also have a series of 20-minute interviews with Academy Members around the country on what's worked in their practice. It's a fascinating series!

We found the easiest way to make these series available is to allow non-members to sign up for the series of courses and participate in the topics they like and skip the ones they are not interested in.

To register for this 8-week long series, go to **http://www.aaepa.com/8weekcourse/**.

Assuming you have no bar complaints or credit issues, that your references check out and the interviewing process you go through with the Academy team gives a green light for Membership, here is a review of some of the areas that will impact your successful implementation:

Have appropriate financing.

Attorneys need to be in a financial position that allows them to build a practice from a *plan*, not a *checkbook balance*. It helps if the attorney brings an entrepreneurial spirit to the table and is also curious and coachable.

Law firm owners need to be in a strong financial position before starting Membership in the Academy. We say this because we have seen attorneys join and operate their practice on a shoestring budget and the pressure takes every ounce of enjoyment out of the journey. "Everything must work, or else," can't be the underlying thought when approaching Membership startup.

Have an unstoppable work ethic.

We are not "the magic bullet"—*you are*. We often say Membership is like a toolbox filled with saws, hammers and nails. Some people take these tools and build a beautiful practice and some attempt to build their practice without the tools we've provided. You can imagine the very different outcomes.

The coaching that goes along with all of the tools in the toolbox is the key. Often we are our own worst enemies. Having a coach who has the permission to tell you if you're getting lost in details or that you're spending too much time tinkering with document language or editing slides instead of building relationships and putting marketing in place means all the difference.

Be coachable and committed.

The first few months spent transitioning all areas of your practice can be overwhelming. You won't be alone. There is an entire team at the Academy available to you and an entire Membership in your corner. Maintaining excitement and staying true to your vision is imperative.

Warning!

Membership is not for the faint of heart. The first 90-120 days are hectic, chaotic and many attorneys doubt their sanity. *But*, if you develop your vision, dream about it at night, work at executing on the activities that bring it all together... it's worth it.

In short, Membership is hard work and we want to be straight about that. Having a track to run on is invaluable, having the tools, the coaching and the support cuts years off of the path to success, but not without a little elbow grease.

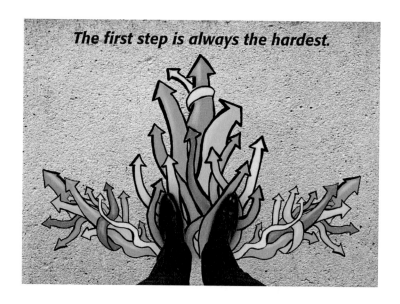

The first step is always the hardest.

You <u>can</u> have the practice you dreamed about.

We have a process that attorneys looking at Membership go through. The process takes time. You can't rush it. You're looking at your current level of satisfaction with your practice and your life—and you absolutely must have clarity about whether or not you want to stay on the track you're on or get off and creates a new path.

Sometimes this process can take weeks. Stick to the process and by the time you work through these steps, you will be able to make a commitment that you either stay on the path you're on or you make a change. Take your time. It's not a race.

No pressure. We're here to help.

Check off the areas that you have completed, and schedule the next step.

☐ Be still and **remember the practice you dreamed about having.** Become very clear about all the details surrounding that firm. The size, the number of attorneys, what the lobby looks like, how many team members you would have, the type of clients you'd work with. And don't forget to include the number of hours you'd work or vacations you would take while working in this dream practice. No one can help you with this step... it's your dream.

☐ **Determine how close you are to living that life.** Consider what is standing in the way of the changes that need to be made in order to have this practice and fulfillment.

☐ **Browse the www.aaepa.com website** and become familiar with the services and Member stories. Daydream a little.

☐ **Request information** (take your pick from the Free Stuff section of this book) and participate on one or two webinars. Feel a tingle of interest, possibility and hope.

☐ **Ponder.** This is a critical step. Review everything, make adjustments to your dream, picture whether or not some of the stories you hear Members talking about could be you.

☐ **Make a list of your doubts.** All of them.

☐ **Email questions@aaepa.com and ask for a phone appointment.** Understand that this call is not a sales call. This is a call about your goals, your doubts and an exploration about whether or not the tools and support we have will help you achieve what you have in mind. The call generally lasts 45 minutes to one hour.

☐ Assuming we can help, you **contact two or three Academy Members.** We're happy to connect you with an attorney you have something in common with. With these Members, you raise every question and doubt possible and be prepared for honest feedback. No holds barred.

- ☐ **We may prescribe one or two webinars.** It's helpful to get a closer look at the software, or marketing approaches or planning techniques and we have a series of replays that may answer some questions you have about the quality of the support Members experience.

- ☐ **Submit an application and find out if you are qualified to attend a Boot Camp as a VIP Guest.** *We waive the entire tuition cost for approved guests. There is no obligation to join.* It is an event that could change everything for you. It isn't required that you attend a Boot Camp as a VIP Guest, but it does give you a complete look behind the curtain before you make a decision. It also gives the Academy team a chance to get to know you.

- ☐ **Yes or no, and no is ok.** You have to make a decision. If you opt to stay on the course you're on, we wish you well. If you choose to become a Member and your application is approved—we get started. *If you don't make a decision then you're guaranteed to stay in the same position.* By making a decision, at the very least, you'll be confident about the direction you choose to take.

Try some of the following stories on for size.

JERRY DORN

Reno, NV
Member Since 1996

"I've been a member of the Academy now for eleven years, and over the years I've investigated numerous membership organizations that represent various court organizations in the estate planning industry, and in fact I'm a member of a number of those still today, including the Academy.

The one thing that I have learned through my detailed investigation of these organizations is that none of them offer a complete turn-key program like the Academy does in terms of providing a different way of looking at your practice from a standpoint of being an entrepreneur focusing on working on your business so you have something of tangible value that you can ultimately transition out of and sell.

Handling all aspects of the management of that business, everything from marketing to HR issues to internal systems and procedures in terms of processing work through your office. In terms of establishing what the organizational structure should look like and actually putting together an organizational chart, complete with detailed job descriptions for each individual position within the framework of the organization.

There's just nothing like it, and then the events getting the consistent support and additional information in terms of what we should be doing, staying cutting-edge in the various areas and staying on top of developments within your organization, and within the industry.

There really are none that touch it, and for those out there who are considering membership and are also considering other organizations, the likelihood is I'm either a member of that organization or have investigated it. Feel free to give me a call and discuss the details of kind of a side-by-side comparison of how the Academy addresses things like no other organization does."

DAN DEBRUYCKERE

New Hampshire and Massachusetts Offices
Member Since 2012

"When I investigated joining the American Academy, I had a general law practice. It was, at some times, a financial struggle. I was looking for a way to create a business model for my law practice. When I finally joined the Academy, it changed my life. I have to say it was the best business decision I ever made.

The Academy provided me with systems, processes, training, and the ability to put together a law firm that provides the financial accomplishments that I was looking for as well as a better life for my team and myself. I now have four offices and it's going really well, thanks to the Academy.

The best part is that it's a business model with benchmarks, so we know when we're doing well and we can monitor on a periodic basis and fix things before they become a problem."

MELANIE LEE

Richmond, VA
Member Since 2006

"I found the Academy one night after my father passed away. I had started my practice and decided at that time that I would take over my father's accounting practice and practice law on the side.

I remember reading the Membership materials and another referral from a Member who said the Academy is a complete solution for the estate planning attorney. I was just looking for estate planning software. What I found was indeed the complete solution. Through the Academy I have become one of the top estate planning attorneys in my area. The tools and systems help you create the practice of your dreams, but more importantly, I've discovered the lifestyle and life that I really want to have. The Membership support you receive is far beyond anything you'll ever find in the marketplace or on this side of the practice of law. We've made friendships beyond compare and have received support that we could have never imagined."

JEFF COOPER

Rutherfordton, NC
Member Since 2013

"I joined the Academy as a general practitioner. I knew that I wanted to focus on estate planning to capitalize on the strength of my being an attorney and a CPA. When I found the Academy, I knew it was a good fit because of the education programs they had, and I knew I was going to need some mentorship to get into the estate planning area exclusively. What I found, really, was beyond my expectations. The first thing I noticed at the first Academy event I attended was how collegiate the entire group is, from the founders all the way down through the Membership. Everyone wants to help in any way they can. You don't see that level of professionalism with attorneys, so it was a refreshing, incredible experience.

I've added an associate attorney, my team has doubled in size, we've opened two satellite offices to service a larger area, and I couldn't be more pleased with the results. In the first two years of my Membership, we had over 90% revenue growth both of those years. I couldn't be more pleased. I'm really grateful to Robert and Sandy for pioneering this group and putting something together that all of us love so much. I highly recommend the Academy if you want to systematize your practice and grow your practice in a way that's sustainable and have a great group of people to do it with."

JACK ALPERN

Boardman, OH
Member Since 1993

"Honestly, besides the practice management, business building, marketing efforts and a wonderful education department that the Academy offers, I think the most valuable asset that the Academy offers is the collegiality that almost for eternity like atmosphere of the members. I can honestly say that I'm usually a loner but some of the best friends I have in the world right now are fellow Academy members. I know I could call them anytime day or night and get the help that I need and the reason I know that is because I've done that and they've called me. The books are open, they'll talk about the numbers, how much income they make, how much expenses they incur, they'll give you ideas that have worked and just as importantly ideas that have not worked.

It's the most amazing group of individuals I have ever encountered. Not only have I never encountered a bunch of lawyers that act this way, I'm never encountered any kind of professional group of any kind that acts that way.

The meetings in the hallways that I have at the Academy events, the chatting in between the breaks, the round table discussions that we have, where people are not only giving up themselves and their expertise but they also give of themselves in a very personal way and say what the Academy membership has meant for them.

I can tell you that it's like having 140 partners in a practice and I know that when I call a lawyer who is an Academy member, he's going to either take that call immediately or get back to me the same day of not the same hour. It is just frankly the most incredible group of human beings I've ever encountered and it's just gets better.

The other thing about the Academy membership that's amazing is where people are competitors even in the same territories. They want to see each other do well, they actually applaud when somebody gives a success story at one of the events, they tell you how happy they are for your success and they really mean it. Members of the Academy have an absolutely contributed to my success and I'm proud to say that I've had a rare and humbling opportunity that I hopefully contribute to have contributed to theirs. Anyone who's on the line who wants or needs to think through whether membership is for you or not for you, frankly member isn't for everyone and I think that's a good thing because we're small group of around 135 firms in 44 states, they were going on a specific direction with our firms and sometimes that doesn't line up with where various attorneys calling to chat about things are going, and that's okay.

I want to make one thing abundantly clear, my membership in the Academy has been incredibly helpful to me and my relationship with Academy members has been absolutely invaluable. They are just a unique group of entrepreneurial lawyers around the country but not only that, they're just really good people and they're willing to help anybody who needs help. Masterminds, the Academy has got about 143 of them. They all have something to contribute and most importantly they all do. I'm proud to say I'm a member and I couldn't be wherever I am right now without the assistance of the academy and its membership."

MARK EGHRARI

Smithtown, NY
Member Since 1995

"Leadership to me is, first, having a vision for where we're going and then finding the right people to help bring the law firm to that vision.

I've been a Member of the Academy since 1995. I originally started my practice in 1988. So I've had access to the Academy's support and expertise for over 20 years.

When think about my early legal career, I think first about the fact that, as an entrepreneur, as someone who's running a law firm, I wasn't giving much thought to where we were going. I was really just locked into what was happening at the moment, often putting out fires, often having a pretty stressful day. When I came to the Academy, my eyes were opened to all sorts of things that I had never thought about. I wasn't a bad entrepreneur, in fact I was pretty good. I was more successful than most. But the benefit of the Academy systems, the mentoring and coaching I got from my Practice Building Consultant, really helped focus my firm to achieve things that I never thought possible. Leadership means growing the firm and having the team there to help me accomplish the vision. When I think about what's most valuable about our law firm, it's the services we provide to clients, the huge change that we make in people's lives. Families come to us and we help with the planning, and we help when things are not going well. That's really important, I'll say even sacred work, so finding the right people becomes critically important.

I'm proud to say that I now have 12 full time employees and the ability to motivate them and for them to share in my vision. We're accomplishing really great things."

CHERYL DAVID

Greensboro, NC
Member Since 1997

"I came to my first Boot Camp after seeing some literature and thinking this was too good to be true. I called about 15 attorneys who all reiterated that everything I was hearing and reading about the Academy was true. So I made the trip to that first Boot Camp to see what this group was about.

At that time I had a little baby. I now have three kids. I remember everybody in my family saying, 'You shouldn't do this. Stay at your safe job. Be a litigator.' But litigation wasn't where my heart was. I needed to find something that really spoke to my soul. Where I could meet with families and really make a difference without all the fighting and litigation. In litigation, I've never seen anyone who is totally happy. If you win, that's great, but people didn't get enough or it didn't turn out right. And if you lose, you know what happens then.

The Academy has given me the systems to start my own office. Everything from templates to education, marketing, how to do seminars, adding financial services to my office, Medicaid, writing blogs and optimizing my business online... You name it, this group provides it. Out of everything I've done in my legal career, this has been my favorite opportunity. Each year I grow with it. I'd encourage any attorney considering it to give it a try."

CHRIS GAUGHAN AND CASEY CONNEALY

Overland Park, KS
Members Since 2012

"We were both doing litigation for many years in Kansas City. We enjoyed it and were good at it, but felt like something was missing. It felt like other people were controlling our calendars and we couldn't do the things we wanted to do. We didn't have enough time for our families and we didn't know what our trajectory was.

We were invited to attend an Academy Boot Camp. We were very reluctant at first, but at the event we got fired up, we learned a lot from Robert and Sandy and the Members. We met a lot of attorneys who were actually happy. They had clients who wanted their services, hugged them when they left, and sent them thank you notes. Everyone at the event was very welcoming. It seemed to be a really good change for us and our practice to move forward with something different and rewarding. In litigation, it always cost too much and took too long, and our clients were never happy.

We both have wives and young children. The practice that we had was very chaotic, not a consistent calendar at all. We were looking for a way to replace the income that we had with a schedule that was more flexible and family friendly. That was the first straw that got us to look at this. Frankly, we just fell in love with it.

Going through the Academy's systems, it truly was transformational. It's something that you won't find anywhere else. It has been absolutely wonderful for our firm and for our personal lives. It's nice to have clients who give you a hug at the end of the process and really appreciate what you do for them."

MIKE ROBINSON

Naples, NY
Member Since 1993

"I've been a Member of the Academy since 1993. Before I came out for my initial Boot Camp, I had some reservations. I didn't know whether I even wanted to look into Membership further, but I knew there was no obligation, so why not go investigate a little further.

What I found really opened my eyes to what the possibilities of my practice could be. Not only the educational support, but the marketing support and practice management systems and I can honestly say that not only has my practice been transformed, but consequently my life has been transformed, as well. I'm having more fun in my practice than ever before and I have more time with my family. I encourage anyone on the fence to at least investigate, ask the hard questions. I think you'll find that your trip will be worthwhile."

CALIFORNIA MEMBER

"The Academy has proven invaluable to me. What I find most beneficial about the Academy is that it has provided me a structure for not only the marketing of my law firm, but for the operation of the firm.

One of the services that the Academy provides me is a Practice Building Consultant. No greater benefit can you have than to have someone who is able to look at your practice objectively and point out the things that you don't see because you're working in the practice.

The Academy gives me the wherewithal to work on my practice as well as in it, and I'm very grateful for that and I don't know where else I would have been able to get that kind of support."

NEW JERSEY MEMBER

"We've been Members of the Academy since 1994. The Academy's Education Department is very important to us. My partners and I are all CPAs and we all have advanced degrees in taxation, but the Academy Education Department is just beyond belief.

When we go to regular Bar Association meetings and they say, 'Do your documents include this?' and, 'Do your documents include that?' we always say yes, because the Academy keeps us up-to-date with all the most current documents and knowledge about what's going on in tax law. We're truly state of the art."

WASHINGTON MEMBER

"I've been a Member since 1994. The Academy has been great for me, I have a background in estate planning so the education part has been good, but that wasn't as important to me as the marketing side of the business.

The Academy was able to give me the marketing tools to build an exclusive estate planning practice, and of course the Academy does have territories, but the other Members in the Academy are very good about sharing their ideas with each other because they don't compete directly with each other. I've been able to put together a very successful estate planning practice with thousands of clients."

ILLINOIS MEMBER

"Two things that have always come back to me that mean a lot about the Academy and to our clients is number one; if we don't serve people, if we don't serve clients to the best of our ability, our job satisfaction is basically non-existent. At least, with me.

But also, we have to be happy with what we do. I mean, if I don't get up in the morning and have some energy to go to the office, I'm here to tell you, I'm not going to do a very good job for most of my clients. The Academy has allowed me many avenues of improving the quality of my work for clients, follow-through for the clients, staff training and top quality education.

Above all of the rest, the Members of the Academy support each other, and they challenge each other. When was the last time you went to a Bar Association meeting and the attorneys couldn't stop talking about how much success and enjoyment they were having from their practice. It happens to me every year, twice a year, when I go to the Academy Summit meetings."

MISSOURI MEMBER

"I've been a Member of the Academy since May of 1995. Before then most of my practice was in commercial and business and construction litigation.

I had done a lot of estate planning but never like the Academy. The Academy taught me not only how to be a great estate planner but to be a business person, to know how to run a business, to train a team and lead a team, and it's been really transformative in my professional practice and in my life and certainly in my finances.

I'm deeply appreciative, and I recommend that anybody who's interested in getting out of a rut with their practice consider joining the Academy."

VIRGINIA MEMBER

"I was moved to share a recent story from my practice. I am sure you hear things like this all the time but I still wanted to share. As a new attorney (new to the practice of law and new to estate planning), I started my practice with the Academy. I often find myself relying on Education to feel comfortable in assisting clients or anytime something is or even 'feels' new. The end of last year, I had a case that was very different I emailed Education about the client's problem. Not only did I receive an answer back but Steve took time to talk me through the fact pattern and send me fact scenarios to run through with the client not only helping me understand the law but what I needed to do to assist the client and properly draft the document.

Last week, I had a lunch & learn with the advisor who referred the client to us and she commented that without my knowledge she sent the plan and documents to her brokerage company's attorney. They told her that it was the 'most thorough and complete estate work they have seen in years.' Needless to say, the advisor will be sending me additional work in the future.

I am sure you hear things like this all the time but I really appreciate the time all the Academy team takes to invest in our practice and lives and felt compelled to share this story."

WASHINGTON MEMBER

"I started with another member last year. I would say that his Membership in the Academy (since 1994) and his introduction to the Academy was one of the reasons I bought his firm. I appreciate everything about it. In addition, there are some other things I've done. I've practiced law for about 28 years actively, and I've never been in an organization where the attorneys talk to each other as freely and openly as they do here. It astonished me when I saw it the first time, now I've just come to appreciate it."

#1 Recommendation is *The E-Myth Attorney*!

Personal and Professional Growth

- The Inside Out Revolution—Michael Neill
- Clarity—Jamie Smart
- The Talent Code—Daniel Coyle
- Hiring for Attitude—Mark Murphy
- Difference—Bernadette Jiwa
- The E-Myth Attorney—Gerber, Armstrong and Fisch
- Getting Things Done—David Allen
- The One Thing—Gary Keller
- Now, Discover Your Strengths—Marcus Buckingham
- Selling the Invisible—Harry Beckwith

Basic Estate Planning

- Academy Training: Core Curriculum I Materials and Recordings—Steve Hartnett
- 2004 CCH Master Estate and Gift Tax Guide—Commerce Clearing House
- The Tools and Techniques of Estate Planning—Stephan R. Leimberg
- Federal Estate and Gift Taxation—Stephens, Maxfield, et al.
- Manning on Estate Planning—Rosenbloom, Manning, et al.
- Simple Wealth, Inevitable Wealth—Nick Murray

Asset Protection

- Academy Training: Asset Protection with Academy Documents—Dennis Sandoval
- Asset Protection: Legal Planning and Strategies—Peter Spero

- Asset Protection Planning Guide: A State of the Art Approach of Estate Planning—Barry Engel and David L. Lockwood

Trust Administration
- Academy Trust Administration Training Series—Dennis Sandoval
- California Trust Administration—Gaw, CEB
- Estate Tax Marital Deduction: BNA Estate, Gifts and Trusts Portfolio 843—Jeffrey N. Pennell

Business Succession
- Academy Training: Buy-Sell Agreements for Farming Businesses—Dennis Sandoval and Steve Hartnett
- Estate Planning for Farms and Other Qualified Family Owned Businesses Under Sections 2032A and 2057—Michael G. Barton and Robert Bellatti

CLT, CLAT, CLUTs, and CRTs
- Academy Training: CLATs and CLUTs—Dennis Sandoval
- Charitable Income Trusts: BNA Estate, Gifts and Trusts Portfolio 866—Donald M. Etheridge, Jr., Esq.
- Academy Training: Core Curriculum II Materials and Recordings (covering Irrevocable Life Insurance Trusts and Charitable Remainder Trusts)—Steve Hartnett
- Charitable Remainder Trusts and Pooled Income Funds: BNA Estate, Gifts and Trusts Portfolio 865—Kathryn A. Bradley and Robert J. Rosepink

- WG&L's Tax Economics of Charitable Giving—Research Institute of America
- The Tools and Techniques of Charitable Planning—Stephan R. Leimberg
- Academy Training: Trusts as Beneficiaries of IRAs-Having Your Cake and Eating It, Too—Steve Hartnett

Elder Law

- Academy Training: The Basics of Medicaid Planning—Dennis Sandoval
- Academy Training: Advising Trustees of Special Needs Trust—Craig Reaves
- Elder Law Portfolio Series—Harry Margolis, Esq.
- Tax, Estate and Financial Planning for the Elderly—David English
- Representing the Elderly: Law and Practice—Thomas D. Begley, Jr. and Jo-Anne H. Jeffreys

FLPS

- Academy Training: Family Limited Partnerships and Family Limited Liability Companies: Recent Developments in FLP and FLLC Planning—Dennis Sandoval and Steve Hartnett
- Academy Training: FLP Case Law Update and Drafting FLPs in Light of Recent IRS Victories—Dennis Sandoval and Steve Hartnett
- Academy Training: Sale to Intentionally Defective Grantors Trusts; Basics of Dynasty Trusts—Dennis Sandoval and Steve Hartnett

- Family Limited Partnerships and Family Limited Liability Companies: BNA Estate, Gifts and Trusts Portfolio 812—Louis A. Mezzulo

General
- Tax Planning for Family Wealth Transfers—Howard M. Zaritsky

Income Taxation of Trusts and Beneficiaries
- Income Taxation of Fiduciaries and Beneficiaries—Byrle M. Abbin, CPA
- Federal Income Taxation of Estates and Trusts—Howard M. Zaritskky, Norman Lane and Robert Danforth

Post Mortem Planning
- Post Mortem Tax Planning—Benton Strauss and Jerry Kasner
- Academy Training—IRC 2013: The Credit for Tax on Prior Transfers, An Often Overlooked Post Mortem Planning Strategy that Yields Significant Estate Tax Savings

Preparation of Estate Tax and Fiduciary Tax Returns
- Academy Training: Preparing the 706—Dennis Sandoval and Steve Hartnett
- The Federal Estate Tax: Preparation of the 706—E. Bennett Bolton
- PPCs 706/709 Deskbook—Practitioner's Publishing Company

- PPCs 1041 Deskbook—Practitioner's Publishing Company

QPRTs

- Academy Training: QPRTs—Dennis Sandoval
- Partial Interests—GRATs, GRUTs, QPRTs (Section 2702): BNA Estate, Gifts and Trusts Portfolio 836—Jonathan G. Blattmachr

Retirement

- Life and Death Planning for Retirement Benefits— Natalie B. Choate

ROBERT ARMSTRONG, J.D.
PRESIDENT

American Academy of Estate Planning Attorneys

Robert Armstrong is Co-Founder and President of the American Academy of Estate Planning Attorneys. Robert is a visionary, innovator, and gifted conceptual thinker who has practiced law for more than 35 years. For the past two decades, he has coached successful entrepreneurial attorneys to have a balanced life and record breaking revenues.

In 2010, he co-authored *The E-Myth Attorney, Why Most Legal Practices Don't Work and What to Do About It* with small business legend Michael Gerber. This Amazon best-seller shows how forward thinking law firms can systematize their practices and develop unique delivery systems to prosper in an increasingly commoditized world. The following year he co-authored *Dominate Your Market, The Attorney's Complete Guide to Online Marketing and Social Media* to help attorneys effectively use cutting edge strategies to ensure market leadership.

Robert is committed to making the business-savvy practitioner the standard for professional success in estate planning. His philosophies, systems, and strategies help good lawyers become great, satisfied, and successful business owners. The American Academy was inspired by his conviction that attorneys, in order to be successful, need more than just technical legal skills. Today, Robert serves as President of the Academy and is responsible for collaborating on the strategic direction of the organization and overseeing the Academy's Marketing, Technical Support, and Software Development departments.

Several years ago he saw the need for intensive personal coaching for attorneys who wanted accountability and help applying the programs the Academy provides. The elite Peak Performers group was founded with multiple face-to-face sessions and daily accountability. With the aid of his leadership, these dedicated Peak Performers are transforming every aspect of their lives.

Robert has co-authored several other books, including the practice management book for attorneys, *Creating a Loving Trust Practice*, and the books, *Total Wealth Management, Estate Planning Basics: A Crash Course in Safeguarding Your Assets, Dominate Your*

Market, and *Legacy Wealth Planning.* He also contributed his expertise to the bestseller, *Terry Savage on Money.*

Professional Experience

Robert has been a practicing attorney since 1976 and is the founder of one of the most successful estate planning practices in the country. In 1989, he joined forces with fellow estate planning attorney, Sanford Fisch. Together they serve as principals with the San Diego, California law firm, Armstrong, Fisch & Tutoli, where they have created thousands of quality estate plans for grateful clients. In 1993, Robert co-founded the American Academy to help Members build successful and robust practices through a rich array of products, services, and systems. With step-by-step coaching, the Academy helps Members effectively use technology, successfully and ethically market estate planning services, create precise accounting systems, inspire law firm staff, and stay current with the ever-changing estate planning laws.

Education

After four years in the U.S. Navy, including a decorated combat tour of duty in Da Nang, Vietnam, Robert attended the University of California at San Diego, where he graduated summa cum laude with a Bachelor of Arts Degree in Classical Greek. In 1976, Robert earned his Juris Doctor degree from the University of San Diego, where he was a staff writer for the Law Review and was awarded the prestigious American Jurisprudence Award for excellence in Insurance Law. Robert holds Series 7 and 66 Securities Licenses and a California Life Insurance License, ensuring that clients receive the benefits of coordinated estate and financial plans.

Personal

Robert and his wife reside in beautiful San Diego, California. They have four grown children with whom they like to spend as much time as possible. Robert is an insatiable reader and also enjoys watching movies, working out every day, and traveling the world.

SANFORD M. FISCH, J.D., LL.M.
CHIEF EXECUTIVE OFFICER

American Academy of Estate Planning Attorneys

Sanford M. Fisch has spent over 30 years combining his keen business sense with an unparalleled understanding of strategic law firm management, marketing, and client relations. His ardent desire and deep commitment to helping fellow attorneys drove him to co-found the American Academy of Estate Planning Attorneys.

Today, Sanford continues to serve as Chief Executive Officer at the Academy. He is responsible for collaborating on the strategic direction of the Academy, working with Members on strategic planning in their law firms, and increasing firm productivity, as well as building alliances with other organizations which provide resources to Academy Members.

By constantly seeking better and more effective ways of doing things, he continues to make a real difference by transforming law firms, the industry, and lives along the way.

In addition, he is a co-author of *The E-Myth Attorney*, which reflects the vast experience gained over a more than 30 year career in practice, and as an advisor and coach to lawyers throughout the country. Other books he has co-authored include *Total Wealth Management, Estate Planning Basics: A Crash Course in Safeguarding Your Assets, Dominate Your Market,* and *Legacy Wealth Planning.*

Professional Experience

In addition to building a prominent estate planning law firm, and co-founding the Academy, Sanford has used his experience to add the Academy Peak Performers coaching program as well as a special coaching program for effective consultations to his regular duties. Through his work at the Academy, he has become a recognized leader and much sought-after advisor, speaker, and consultant to law firms throughout the United States.

His early career was spent as a Tax Specialist with Coopers and Lybrand, an international accounting firm. He also taught at the American College for Certified Financial Planners and Chartered Underwriters. In 1989, he joined forces with fellow estate planning attorney and Academy co-founder Robert Armstrong and is currently a principal of Armstrong, Fisch & Tutoli, APLC. In 1993, Sanford co-founded the American Academy of Estate Planning Attorneys.

Education

A solid legal education, including a Masters degree in tax law from Georgetown University Law Center in 1982, was the foundation for Sanford's career. He graduated magna cum laude from Boston University in 1977, earning a Bachelor of Science

Degree in Economics, where he was a member of the National Mortar Board Honor Society. In 1980, he went on to earn his law degree from the University of San Diego, where he received the American Jurisprudence Award for excellence in Civil Procedure. He was also published in the Law Review, *"To Be or Not to Be—Tax is the Question?"*

Personal

Sanford is the Co-Founder and former Chairman of the San Diego Senior Olympics. He enjoys golf, surfing, running, hiking, and raising his daughter Tahlia with his wife Julie. The family, along with their 2 dogs, live in the beach community of Pacific Beach.

Made in the USA
San Bernardino, CA
27 October 2017